ABC's for the Moorish American Family

Written and Illustrated by William Osiris Amurru Bey

Text Copyright © 2023 by William Osiris Bey
Illustrations copyright © 2023 by William Osiris Amurru Bey
Edited By: Akilah Trinay
Interior Decorator: Shantelle "Peaches" Harris

All rights reserved. No part of this book may be reproduced–mechanically, electronically or used in any manner, including photocopying–without the prior written permission of the copyright owner, except for the use of brief quotations in a book review. Published in the United States.

Library of Congress Number: 2023916374
ISBNs:
Paperback - 979-8-9890480-0-7
Hardcover - 979-8-9890480-1-4

Books are available at special discounts when purchased in bulk for premiums and sales promotions as well as for fund-raising or educational use.
For details, please contact The Chosen Few Collective LLC at the address below or send an email to: Thechosenfew@mail.com.

The Chosen Few Collective LLC
296 MacArthur Blvd., Suite 144
San Leandro, CA 94577
thechosenfew.storenvy.com

Publishing Consultant:
Revision Publishing LLC
www.revisionpub.com

Dedications & Acknowledgements

I rise high on the 7 giving perfect praise to Allah, the author, the creator the governor of the world the almighty, eternal and incomprehensible. To the one who is supreme, most wise and beneficent, and to Him alone, belong worship, adoration, thanks giving and praise.

I give honors to my illustrious and industrious forefathers Marcus Messiah Garvey and The Prophet Noble Drew Ali.

I give honors to my tribe, friends, and family who helped in creating this book.

Special Honors
Grand Sheikh Cozmo El
Shantelle "Peaches" Harris
Octavia Simms Bohanon
Laniyah Collins-Bey
Akilah Trinay

Aa

ALLAH - Father of the universe. The author, the creator, the governor of the world, almighty, eternal, and incomprehensible. The most supreme, most wise and beneficent and Him alone belong worship, adoration, thanksgiving and praise.

Angel - An angel is a thought of ALLAH manifested in human flesh. Spiritual being attendant upon ALLAH.

Aught - Truth; ALLAH

Asiatic - Belonging to or characteristic of Asia.

Moorish American Astronaut

Asiatic Moor

Bb

Beautiful Benebolent Moorish Beauties

Bey - Surname for Moorish Americans.

Buddha - A true and divine prophet. This philosophical teacher was an ascetic and spiritual teacher of South Asia who lived during the latter half of the first millennium BCE. Buddhists revere the founder of Buddhism as a fully enlightened being who taught a path to Nirvana. Freedom from ignorance, craving, rebirth and suffering.

Benevolence - Disposition to do good. An inclination to do kind or charitable acts. An act intending or showing kindness and good will. One of the ninety-nine names of ALLAH.

Birthright - Is the concept of things being due to a person upon or by the fact of their birth, or because of the order of their birth. These may include rights of citizenship based on a place where the person was born, a citizenship of their parents, and inheritance rights to property owned by parents or others.

Black - According to science, it means death.

Beauty - The qualities that give pleasure to the senses; an outstanding example of its kind.

Cc

Covenant - Mutual compact to do or not do something. A contract, agreement, pact, or promise. To come together, unite. In law, a promise made by deed. Applied to scripture to ALLAH arrangement with man.

Constitution - Law, regulation, edict; body of rules, customs or laws. Establishment; order ordinance, to cause, to stand, set up, fix, place establish, set in order; form something new or resolve.

Charity - Mercy, compassion; alms; costliness, esteem, or affection. An act of kindness or philanthropy. Maintained by voluntary contributions or bequests.

Character - The inherent complex of attributes that determine a person's moral and ethical actions and reaction.

Community - A number of people associated together with the fact of residence in the same locality; the common people; society, fellowship, courtesy, condescension, affability, common, public, general, shared by all or many.

Dd

Divine - Pertaining to, of the nature of, or proceeding from ALLAH or of belonging to ALLAH. Inspired, prophetic, deity; to shine

Diligence - Constant and earnest effort to accomplish what is overtaken. Attention, cares, haste, speed: Attentiveness, carefulness, single out, value highly, esteem, prize, love, aspire to be content with appreciation.

Deity - Divine nature, godhood, attributes of a god. A supreme being or self-existing spirit. A being to whom a divine or godlike nature is attributed.

Descendants - An individual proceeding from an ancestor in any degree, to come down.

Dua - Is a prayer of invocation, supplication or request, even asking for help or assistance from ALLAH.

Moorish American Doctors

Ee

El - Surname for Moorish Americans.

Education - Bring up, to train, lead forth.

Economics - Pertaining to management of a household. The system of production and management of material wealth. Relating to the science of economics.

Everlasting Gospel - It is a saving that comes from ALLAH through our Ancient Fathers, by His Prophet.

Elihu - Teacher of Jesus.

Elizabeth - Mother of John the Baptist.

Father - He who begets a child; the nearest male ancestor; the Supreme Being. One who exercises parental care over another.

Founder - One who establishes, one who sets up institutes something. Originator. To lay the foundation.

Flag - Cloth ensign. Emblems usually consisting of a rectangular piece of cloth of distinctive designs.

Freedom - Power of self-determination, state of free will; emancipation from slavery, deliverance from the condition of being forced; the power to act or speak or think without externally imposed restraints.

Family - Servants of a household, members of household; the estate, property; a social unit living together with a primary social group; parents and children.

Fez - A felt cap (usually red) for a man; shaped like a flat-topped cone, with a tassel that hangs from the crown.

Father

Gg

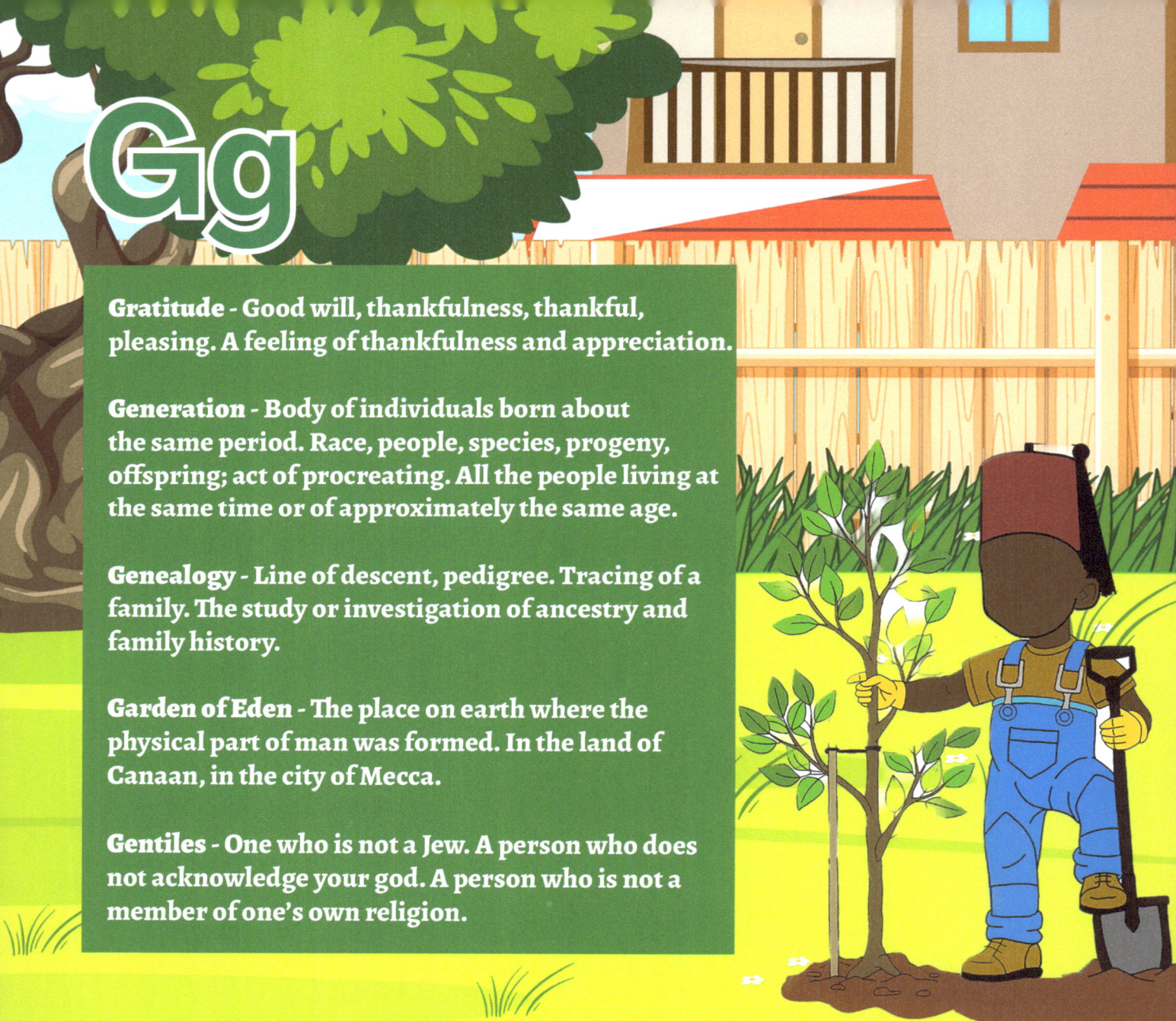

Gratitude - Good will, thankfulness, thankful, pleasing. A feeling of thankfulness and appreciation.

Generation - Body of individuals born about the same period. Race, people, species, progeny, offspring; act of procreating. All the people living at the same time or of approximately the same age.

Genealogy - Line of descent, pedigree. Tracing of a family. The study or investigation of ancestry and family history.

Garden of Eden - The place on earth where the physical part of man was formed. In the land of Canaan, in the city of Mecca.

Gentiles - One who is not a Jew. A person who does not acknowledge your god. A person who is not a member of one's own religion.

Moorish American Gardener

Hh

Health - A healthy state of wellbeing free from disease. The general condition of body and mind.

Husband - A male head of a household, master of a house; householder. A married man; a woman's partner in marriage.

Holy - Consecrated, sacred; godly; ecclesiastical. A sacred place of pilgrimage. Belonging to or derived from or associated with a divine power.

Higher self - The mother of virtues and the harmonies of life and breeds justice, mercy, love and right. ALLAH in man.

Humanity - The quality of being humane. The quality of being human. All the living human inhabitants of the earth.

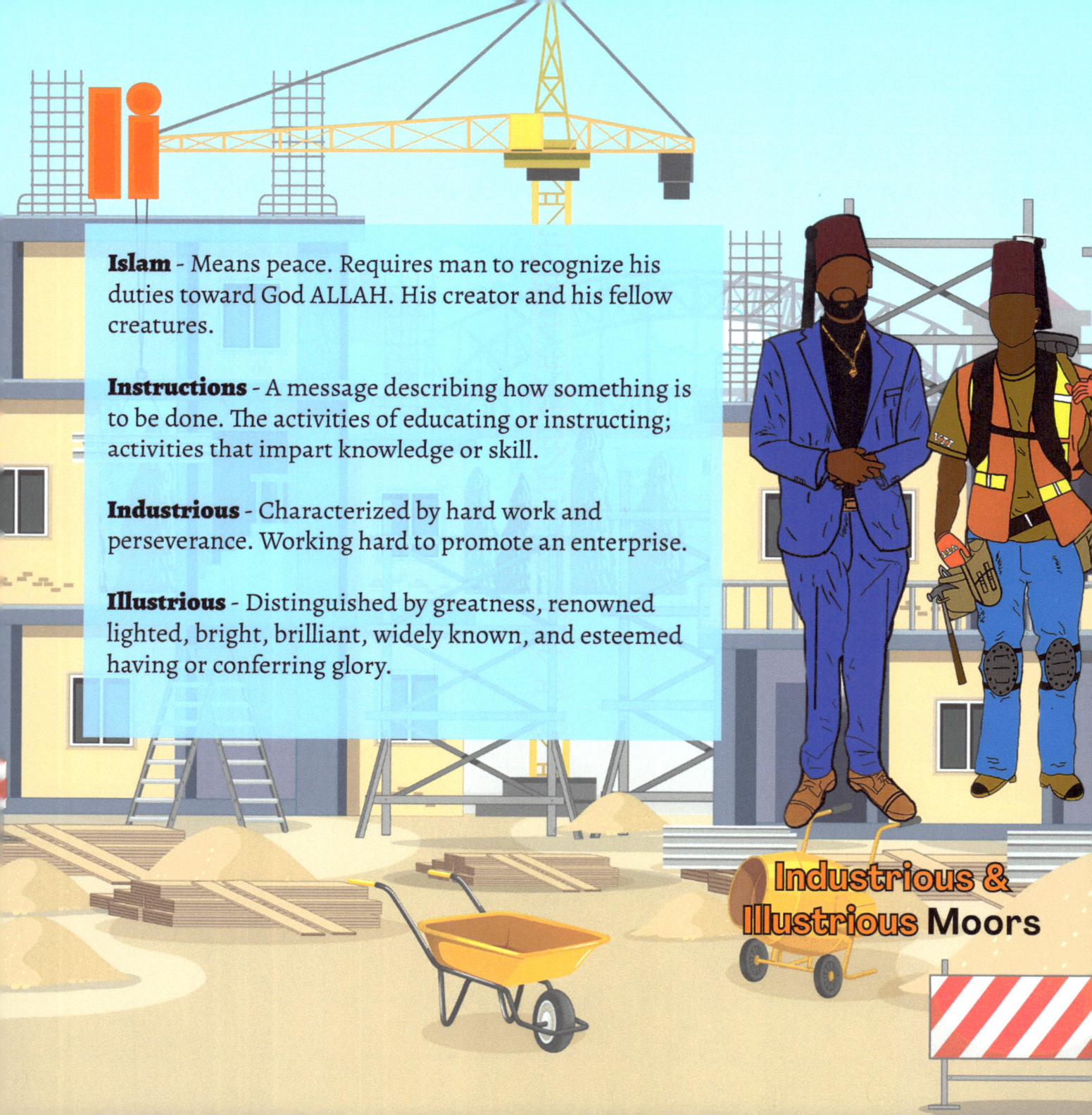

Jj

Justice League

Jesus - A prophet of ALLAH. Jesus means Justice. Son of Joseph and Mary.

Justice - The exercise of authority in vindication of right by assigning reward or punishment. Also, quality of being fair and just, moral soundness and conformity to truth. The quality of being fair or just. Judgment involved in the determination of rights and the assignment of rewards and punishments.

Jurisdiction - The right and power to interpret and apply the law. In law; the territory within which power can be exercised.

Jerusalem - Holy city in ancient Judea, literally "foundation of peace," Holy city for Jews and Christians and Muslims; was the capital of an ancient kingdom.

Judah - (Old Testament) The fourth son of Jacob, who was a forebear of the tribe of Israel; one of his descendants was to be the Messiah. An ancient kingdom of southern Palestine with Jerusalem as its center.

Knowledge - The psychological result of perception and learning and reasoning.

Koran - Which is to be read. Book which contains the Islamic religious and moral code; the standard work of Classical Arabic. Sacred writings of Islam revealed by ALLAH to the prophet Muhammad during his life at Mecca and Medina.

Key - Something crucial for explaining.

Kingdom - A domain in which something is dominant. The domain ruled by a king or queen.

Kaaba - (Islam) A black stone building in Mecca that is shaped like a cube and that is the most sacred Muslim pilgrim shrine; believed to have been given by Gabriel to Abraham. Muslims turn in its direction when praying.

King Mansa Musa

Ll

Love - A strong positive emotion of regard and affection. Any object of warm affection or devotion, a beloved person; used as a term of endearment.

Lessons - A unit of instruction. Punishment intended as a warning to others. The significance of a story or event. A task assigned for individual study.

Lower self - The carnal self, the body of desires. A reflection of higher self, distorted by the murky ethers of the flesh. An illusion that will pass away.

Law - The collection of rules imposed by authority. A legal document setting forth rules governing a particular activity. A generalization that describes recurring facts or events in nature.

Literature - Creative writing of recognized artistic value. Published writings in a particular style on a particular subject.

Mm

Marcus Mosiah Garvey

Moor - Descendant of Morocco born in America.

Mother - A woman who has given birth to a child. A term to address an elderly woman. A condition that is the inspiration for an activity or situation.

Morals - Associated with or characterized by right behavior. Concerned with principles of right and wrong or conforming to standards of behavior and character based on those principles. Psychological rather than physical or tangible, in effect.

Movement - A natural event that involves a change in the position or lactation of something. A group of people with a common ideology who try together to achieve certain general goals.

Marcus Mosiah Garvey - was a Jamaican political activist. He was the founder and first President-General of the Universal Negro Improvement Association. Forerunner to the Prophet, Noble Drew Ali

Nn

Noble - Man of Rank, person of acknowledgment; social or political preeminence; person of rank above commoner. Impressive in appearance. Having or showing or indicative of high or elevated character.

Nationality - People having common origins or traditions and often comprising a nation. The status of belonging to a particular nation by birth or naturalization.

Noble Drew Ali - A Prophet of ALLAH. Founder of the Moorish Science Temple of America. Born in the state of North Carolina 1886.

Noble Drew Ali

Oo

Obedience- the practice or virtue of submission to a higher power or authority. Dutiful compliance with a command or law. The trait of being willing to obey.

Organization- A group of people who work together. An organized structure for arranging or classifying. The act of organizing a business or an activity related to a business.

Oath- solemn promise, usually invoking a divine witness, regarding your future acts or behavior

Obedience

Peace - Harmonious relations; freedom from disputes. The absence of mental slaves or anxiety. A treaty to cease hostilities.

Prudence - Discretion in practical affairs, knowing how to avoid embarrassment or distress.

Prophet - A prophet is a thought of ALLAH manifest in flesh. A person who speaks for ALLAH. One who foretells; inspired preacher. An authoritative person who defines the future.

Purity - Being undiluted or unmixed with extraneous material. The state of being unsullied by sin or moral wrong. Lacking knowledge for evil. Freedom from moral contamination; sinlessness, innocence, righteousness, simple truth.

Proclaim - Make known by public announcement. Declare formally; declare someone to be someone of title.

Qq

Quality - An essential and distinguishing attribute of something or someone; the quality of mercy is not strained. A degree or grade of excellence or worth. A characteristic property that defines the apparent individual nature of something.

Qu'ran - That which is to be read. The sacred writings of Islam revealed by God to the prophet Muhammad during his life at Mecca and Medina.

Rr

Religion - Action or conduct showing a belief in a divine power and reverence for a desire to please it. A firm belief in a supernatural power or power that controls human destiny.

Redeem - Save from sins. Restore the honor or worth of.

Recognize - Accept someone to be what is claimed or accept his power and authority; be fully aware of. Detect with senses.

Ruth - A Moabites.

Real Estate - Real estate is property comprising land and the buildings on it, along with its natural resources such as crops, minerals or water; immovable property of this nature, an interest vested in this an item of real property, buildings or housing.

Reveal - Disclose directly or through prophets. Make known to the public information previously known only to a few people, or that was meant to be kept a secret.

Ruth the Moabitess

Salvation - The saving of the soul; deliverance from the power of sin, and admission to eternal bliss. The act of delivering from sin or saving from evil. A means of preserving from harm or unpleasantness.

Sincerity - An earnest and sincere feeling. The quality of being open and truthful, not deceitful or hypocritical. A quality of naturalness and simplicity.

Spirit - The vital principles or animating force within living things.

Soul - The immaterial part of a person; the actuating cause of an individual life. The personality of a man. A substantial entity believed to be that in each person which lives, feels, thinks and wills.

Science - State or fact of knowing; what is known, knowledge gained by study; information; assurance of knowledge.

Sisters Auxiliary

Tt

Truth - Faith; faithfulness, fidelity, loyal, veracity, quality of true; pledge, covenant. A fact that has been verified. Conformity to reality or actuality.

Temperance - Self- restraint, moderation, sobriety, discretion, self- control.

Temple - Building for worship, edifice dedicated to the service of a deity or deities. Place of worship consisting of an edifice for the worship of a deity.

Time - An instance or single occasion for some event. An indefinite period (usually marked by specific attributes or activities). A suitable moment.

Testimony - A solemn statement made under oath. An assertion offering firsthand authentication of a fact.

Turban - A traditional Muslim headdress consisting of a long scarf wrapped around the head.

Uu

Unity - State or property of being one. An individual or unbroken completeness or totality with nothing wanting; oneness, sameness, agreement.

Understanding - Comprehension; mutual agreement, the cognitive condition of someone who understands. An inclination to support or be loyal to or to agree with an opinion. Characterized by understanding based on comprehension and discernment and empathy.

Uplifting - Fill with high spirits; fill with optimism. Lift from the earth, as by geologic forces; elevate.

Universal Allah - Wisdom, Will, Love.

UNITING

Vv

Virtue - Moral life and conduct; a particular moral excellence; force, strength, vigor; moral; strength; qualities, abilities. The quality of doing what is right and avoiding what is wrong.

Vanity - Futile, or worthless; self-conceit, lack of resolve; feeling of excessive pride. The quality of being valveless or futile. The trait of being unduly vain and conceited; false pride

Veterinarian Moors

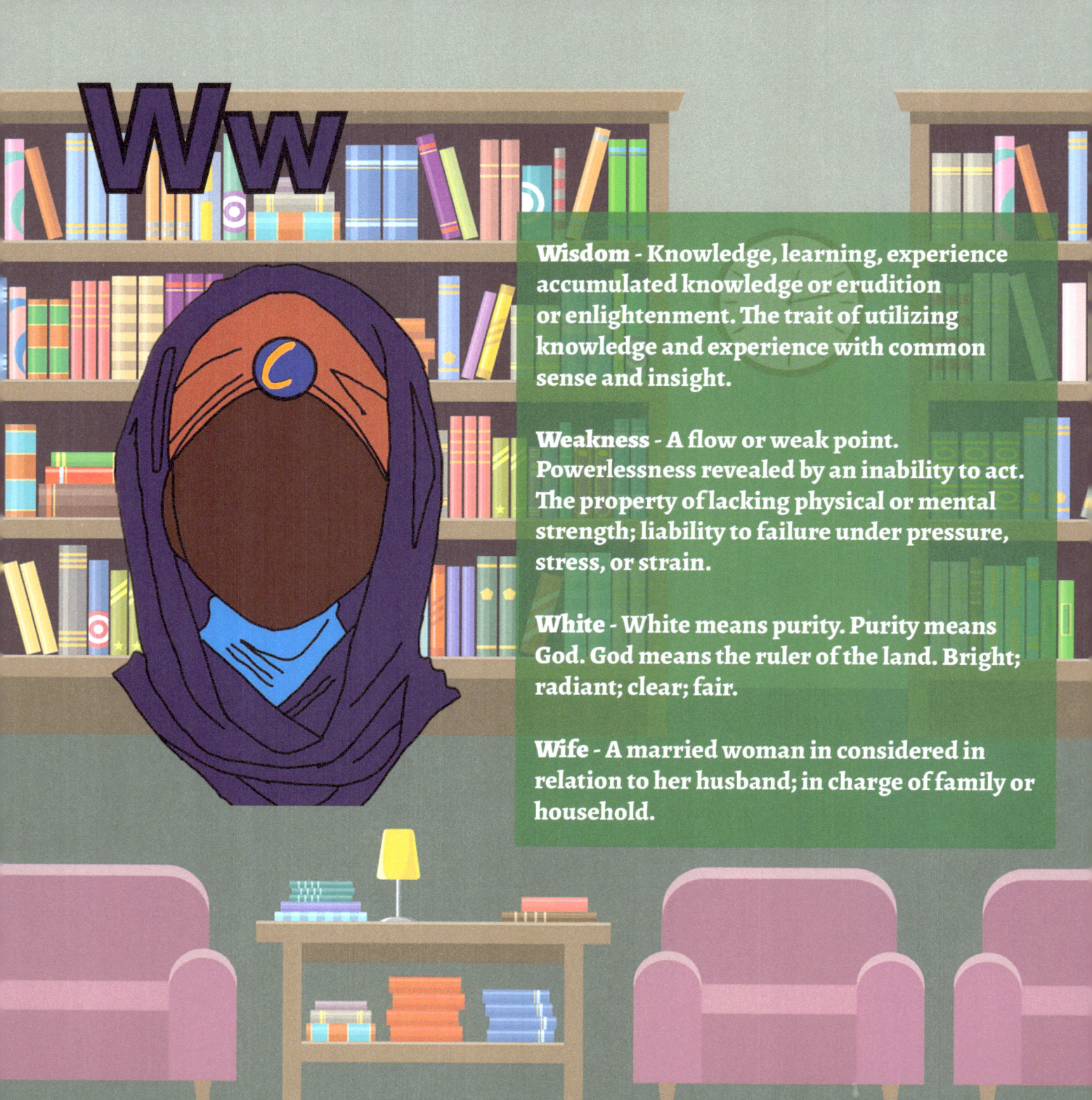

Zz

Zakat- The 4th pillar of Islam is almsgiving as an act of worship.

Zodiac- A belt-shaped region in the heavens on either side to the ecliptic; divided into 12 constellation or signs for astrological purpose.

ABOUT THE AUTHOR

Greetings, my name is William Osiris Amurru Bey, and I proudly claim Oakland, California as my birthplace and hometown. I am honored to be a member of the esteemed Moorish Science Temple of America California No. 1, where I have held the esteemed position of Assistant Grand Sheikh for a remarkable two-year spell.

The creation of this book stemmed from a dual purpose - to serve as an enriching literary work and a comprehensive study guide for Moorish American families. Its goal is to empower individuals to delve into their national heritage and Divine Creed. Rooted in the teachings of our esteemed and revered Noble Prophet Drew Ali, this book seeks to heed his counsel for active Moors to cultivate industriousness and distinction.

With utmost sincerity, I hope this book thrives as a beacon, illuminating and uplifting humanity. May peace and love reign supreme.

Divine Constitution & Bi-Laws

SALVATION ALLAH UNITY

The Divine Constitution of Moorish Science Temple of America

Act 1 - The Grand Sheik and the Chairman of Moorish Science Temple of America is in power to make law and enforce laws with the assistance of the Prophet and the Grand Body of Moorish
Science Temple of America. The Assistant Grand Sheik is to assist the Grand Sheik in all affairs if he lives according to Love, Truth, Peace, Freedom and Justice, and it is known before the members of Moorish America.

Act 2 - All meetings are to be opened and closed promptly according to the Circle Seven and Love, Truth, Peace, Freedom and Justice. Friday is our Holy Day of rest, because on a Friday the first man was formed in flesh and on a Friday the first man departed out of flesh and ascended unto his Father God Allah, for that cause Friday is the Holy Day for all Moslems all over the world.

Act 3 - Love, Truth, Peace, Freedom and Justice must be proclaimed and practiced by all members of Moorish Science Temple of America. No member is to put in danger or accuse falsely His Brother or Sister on any occasion at all that may harm His Brother or Sister, because Allah is Love.

Act 4 - All members must preserve these Holy and Divine laws, and all members must obey the laws of the Government, because by being a Moorish American, you are a part and partial of this said government, and must live the life accordingly.

Act 5 - This organization of the Moorish Science Temple of America is not to cause any confusion or to overthrow the Laws and Constitution of the said government but to obey hereby.

Act 6 - With us all members must proclaim their nationality and we are teaching our people their nationality and their Divine Creed that they may know that they are a part and a partial of this said government, and know that they are not Negroes, Colored Folks, Black People or Ethiopians, because these names were given to slaves by slave holders in 1779 and lasted until 1865 during the time of slavery; but this is a New Era of time now and all men now must proclaim their free National Name to be recognized by the government in which they live and the nations of the earth. This is the reason why Allah, the Great God of the universe, ordained Noble Drew Ali, the Prophet, to redeem his people from their sinful ways. The Moorish Americans are the descendants of the ancient Moabites whom inhabited the North Western and South Western shores of Africa.

Act 7 - All members must promptly attend their meetings and become a part and a partial of all uplifting acts of the Moorish Science Temple of America. Member must pay their dues and keep in line with all necessities of Moorish Science Temple of America and then you are entitled to the name of "Faithful". Husband, you must support your wife and children; wife you must obey your husband and take care of your children and look after the duties of your household. Sons and daughters must obey father and mother and be industrious and become a part of the uplifting of fallen humanity. All Moorish Americans must keep their hearts and minds pure with love and their bodies clean with water. This Divine Covenant is from your Holy Prophet Noble Drew Ali, thru the guidance of His Father God Allah.

MOORISH AMERICAN PRAYER
Allah the Father of the universe, the Father of Love, Truth, Peace, Freedom and Justice. Allah is my protector, my guide and my salvation by night and by day, thru his Holy Prophet Drew Ali, "Amen

101 Questions for Moorish Children

1. Who made you? ALLAH.
2. Who is ALLAH? ALLAH is the Father of the Universe.
3. Can we see Him? No.
4. Where is the nearest place we can meet Him? In the heart.
5. Who is Noble Drew Ali? He Is Allah's Prophet.
6. What is a Prophet? A Prophet is a thought of ALLAH manifested in flesh.
7. What is the duty of a Prophet? To save nations from the wrath of ALLAH.
8. Who is the founder of the MOORISH SCIENCE TEMPLE OF AMERICA? Noble Drew Ali.
9. What year was the MOORISH SCIENCE TEMPLE OF AMERICA founded? 1913 A.D.
10. Where? Newark, New Jersey.
11. Where was Noble Drew Ali born? In the State of North Carolina, 1886.
12. What is his nationality? Moorish American.
13. What is your nationality? Moorish American.
14. Why are we Moorish Americans? Because we are descendants of Moroccans and born in America.
15. For what purpose was the Moorish Science Temple of America founded? For the uplifting of fallen humanity.
16. How did the Prophet begin to uplift the Moorish Americans? By teaching them to be themselves.
17. What is our religion? Islamism.
18. Is that a new, or is that the old time religion? Old time religion.
19. What kind of a flag is the Moorish? It is a red flag with a five pointed green star in the center.
20. What do the five points represent? Love, Truth, Peace, Freedom and Justice.
21. How old is our flag? It is over 50,000 years old.
22. Which is our Holy Day? Friday.
23. Why? Because Friday is the day on which man was formed in flesh, and it was on Friday when he departed out of flesh.
24. Who was Jesus? He was a Prophet of Allah.
25. Where was He born? In Bethlehem, of Judah, in the house of David.
26. Who were His Father and Mother? Joseph and Mary.
27. Will you give in brief the line (genealogy) through which Jesus came? Some of the Great Fathers through which Jesus came are: Abraham, Boaz by Ruth, Jesse, King David, Solomon, Hezekiah and Joseph by Mary.
28. Why did ALLAH send Jesus to this earth? To save the Israelites from the iron hand oppression of the pale-skin nations of Europe, who were governing a portion of Palestine at that time.
29. How long has that been? About two thousand years ago.
30. What was the nationality of Ruth? Ruth was a Moabites.
31. What is the modern name for the Moabites? Moroccans.
32. Where is the Moroccan Empire? Northwest Amexem.

33. What is the modern name for Amexem? Africa.
34. What is the title given to our ruler in Morocco {East}? Sultan.
35. Where do we get the name Jesus? From the East.
36. What does the name Jesus mean? Jesus means Justice.
37. Did the Angel give to the Child that was called Jesus a Holy Name? Yes, but it cannot be used by those who are slaves to sin.
38. What is an Angel? An Angel is a thought of ALLAH manifested in human flesh.
39. What are Angels used for? To carry messages to the four corner of the world, to all nations.
40. What is our Prophet to us? He is an Angel of ALLAH, who is sent to bring us the Everlasting Gospel of ALLAH.
41. What is the Everlasting Gospel? It is a Saving Power that comes from Allah through our ancient Father, by His Prophet.
42. What is the Covenant of the Great GOD-ALLAH? Honor thy Father and thy Mother, that thy days may be longer upon the Earth land which the Lord thy GOD ALLAH hath given thee.
43. At what age did Jesus begin to teach? At the age of twelve.
44. Where did He teach? India, Africa and Europe.
45. How long did He teach? Eighteen years.
46. What did Jesus say that would make you free? Truth.
47. What is Truth? Truth is Aught.
48. What is Aught? Aught is ALLAH.
49. Can Truth change? TRUTH cannot change, or pass away.
50. What other name do we give to TRUTH? Holy Breath.
51. What have you to say about HOLY BREATH? All we can say is it is Great. It is good. It was, it is, and evermore to be. AMEN.
52. At what place on earth was the physical part of MAN formed? In the Garden of Eden.
53. Where is the Garden of Eden? In the land of Canaan, in the City of Mecca.
54. What is the modern name for the Garden of Eden? MECCA.
55. What is the name of the first physical man? His name cannot be used, only by Executive Rulers of the A.C. of the M.S.T. of A.
56. What are the words of A.C. of the M.S.T. of A.? Adept Chamber of the Moorish Science Temple of America (3rd Heaven).
57. Who were Adam and Eve? They are the mothers and fathers of the human family. Asiatics and Europeans.
58. Where did they go? They went into Asia.
59. What is the modern name given to the children? Asiatics.
60. Who is guarding the Holy City of MECCA today to keep unbelievers away? Angels.
61. What is the modern name for these Angels? Asiatics.
62. What is the shade of their skin? Olive.
63. Are the Moorish Americans any relation to those Angels? Yes, we all have the same father and mother.
64. Give five names that are given to the descendants of Adam and Eve: Lucifer, Satan, Devil, Dragon and Beast.
65. What is the Devil sometimes called? The Lower-self.
66. How many selves are there? Two.
67. Name them: Higher-self and Lower-self.
68. What people represent the Higher-self? The Angels who protect the Holy City of MECCA.
69. What people represent the Lower-self? Those who were cast out of the Holy City, and those who accept their teachings.
70. What is the Higher-self? The Higher-self is the Mother of virtues and the harmonies of life, and breeds Justice, Mercy, Love and Right.

71. Can the Higher-self pass away? No.
72. Why? Because it is ALLAH in MAN.
73. What does the Lower-self breed? Hatred, Slander, Lewdness, Murders, Theft, and everything that harms.
74. What did the Higher-self say to the Lower-self at one time when He met Satan? "Where are you going Satan?"
75. What was the answer that the Lower-self gave to the Higher-self? "I am going to and fro the earth seeking whom I may devour."
76. Has he finished his task of devouring? Yes.
77. When was His time declared out? When He nailed Jesus to the cross.
78. What were the last words Jesus uttered? It is finished.
79. What did He have reference to? He had reference to the end of Satan.
80. Did Jesus say that He would return to conquer Him? Yes.
81. What is the first name of the person into whom Jesus was first reincarnated? Prophet MOHAMMED, the Conqueror.
82. Was Satan to be bound then? Satan was bound in part.
83. When was the head of Satan taken off? 453 (Byzantine).
84. By whom? By Mohammed.
85. Name some of the marks that were put upon the MOORS of Northwest, by the European nations in 1774? Negro, Black, colored and Ethiopian.
86. Negro, a name given to a river in West Africa by MOORS, because it contained black water.
87. What is meant by the word Black? Black according to science means death.
88. What does the word colored mean? Colored means anything that has been painted, varnished or dyed.
89. What does Ethiopian mean? Ethiopia means something divided.
90. Can a man be a Negro, Black, Colored or Ethiopian? No.
91. Why? Because man is made in the Image and after the likeness of God, ALLAH.
92. What title does Satan give Himself? God.
93. Will you define the word White? White means Purity, Purity means God, and God means the Ruler of the Land.
94. To whom do we refer at times, as being the GREAT GOD? ALLAH.
95. Is the Devil made in the Image and Likeness of ALLAH? No, he is the shadow of our lower-selves and will pass away.
96. Who made the Devil? Elohim.
97. Who is Elohim? Elohim is the Seven Creative Spirits that created everything that ever was, is, and evermore to be.
98. What is Elohim sometimes called? The SEVEN EYES of ALLAH.
99. How many days are in the Circle? Seven days.
100. How many days are in a creation? Seven days.
101. According to Science, how many days are in a year? Seven days.

www.ingramcontent.com/pod-product-compliance
Lightning Source LLC
Chambersburg PA
CBHW040723060526

44119CB00083B/307